D1268401

Position and Issues Statements of the Accounting Education Change Commission

**Accounting Education
Change Commission and
American Accounting Association**

Accounting Education Series, Volume No. 13

FLORIDA STATE
UNIVERSITY LIBRARIES

FEB 19 1999

TALLAHASSEE, FLORIDA

HF
5630
.P67
1996

Copyright, Accounting Education Change Commission and
American Accounting Association, 1996
All rights reserved.

ISBN 086539-081-9
Printed in the United States of America

American Accounting Association
5717 Bessie Drive
Sarasota, Florida 34233

Foreword

The mission of the Accounting Education Change Commission (AECC) is to improve the academic preparation of accountants, so that entrants to the profession will possess the skills, knowledge, and values and attitudes required for success in accounting career paths. This mission is consistent with the objectives of the American Accounting Association's "Bedford Committee" report and the Sponsoring Firms' white paper, *"Perspectives on Education: Capabilities for Success in the Accounting Profession."*

The AECC has undertaken a number of initiatives to carry out its charge, including the publication of two position statements and six issues statements. The purpose of this publication is to provide a convenient resource document for all of these publications. Because the AECC was established as an entity of limited life, originally five years and subsequently extended to slightly over seven years, we felt that the AAA Accounting Education Series would be the appropriate ongoing source for this material. We sincerely hope that this information is useful to you in your efforts to enhance the quality of accounting education.

Richard E. Flaherty
Executive Director
Accounting Education Change Commission
Tempe, Arizona
August 1996

Michael A. Diamond
Director of Education
American Accounting Association
Sarasota, Florida
August 1996

OBJECTIVES OF EDUCATION FOR ACCOUNTANTS

Accounting Education Change Commission
Position Statement No. One

September 1990

OBJECTIVES OF EDUCATION FOR ACCOUNTANTS

CONTENTS

The Accounting Education Change Commission was appointed in 1989 by the American Accounting association and supported by the Sponsors' Education Task Force, representing the largest public accounting firms in the United States. Its objective is to be a catalyst for improving the academic preparation of accountants so that entrants to the accounting profession possess the skills, knowledge, and attitudes required for success in accounting career paths. This document may be copied without restriction.

OBJECTIVES OF EDUCATION FOR ACCOUNTANTS

The purpose of this Statement is to set out the Commission's views on the objectives of education for accountants. The Commission believes such a statement will provide a focus for those participating in the work of improving accounting education.

The Commission's aim is to enlist the cooperation and creativity of the academic community and other stakeholders to bring about needed changes in accounting education. The need for changes has arisen because accounting programs have not kept pace with the dynamic, complex, expanding, and constantly changing profession for which students are being educated. The need has been documented in "Future Accounting Education: Preparing for the Expanding Profession" (the Bedford Committee Report) and "Perspectives on Education: Capabilities for Success in the Accounting Profession".

The Commission defines the accounting profession broadly. It includes career paths in public accounting as practiced in large, medium, and small firms, corporate accounting (including financial management, controllership, treasury, financial analysis, planning and budgeting, cost accounting, internal audit, systems, tax, and general accounting), and government and nonprofit accounting.

DESIRED CAPABILITIES

Accounting programs should prepare students to **become** professional accountants, not to **be** professional accountants at the time of entry to the profession. At the time of entry, graduates cannot be expected to have the range of knowledge and skills of experienced professional accountants. To attain and maintain the status of a professional accountant requires continual learning. Therefore, pre-entry education should lay the base on which life-long learning can be built. In other words, graduates should be taught how to learn. The base on which life-long learning is built has three components: skills, knowledge, and professional orientation.

Skills

To become successful professionals, accounting graduates must possess communication skills, intellectual skills, and interpersonal skills. Communication skills include both receiving and transmitting information and concepts, including effective reading, listening, writing, and speaking. Intellectual skills include the ability to locate, obtain, and organize information and the ability to identify and solve unstructured problems in unfamiliar settings and to exercise judgment based on comprehension of an unfocused set of facts. Interpersonal skills include the ability to work effectively in groups and to provide leadership when appropriate.

Knowledge

Accounting graduates should have general knowledge, organizational and business knowledge, and accounting knowledge. General knowledge will help accounting professionals to understand the complex interdependence between the profession and society and to interact with diverse groups of people. Such general knowledge should include an appreciation of the flow of ideas and events in history, an awareness of the different cultures and socio-political forces in today's world, a broad understanding of mathematics and economics, and an aesthetic sensibility. It will lead to an improved understanding of the world-wide economic, political, and social forces affecting society and the profession.

Professional accountants must understand the work environments found in organizations. They must understand the basic internal workings of organizations and the methods by which organizations change. Because organizations are affected by rapidly increasing dependency on technology, accounting professionals must understand the current and future roles of information technology in organizations.

A strong fundamental understanding of accounting is necessary for successful accounting careers. This understanding includes 1) the ability to identify goals, problems, and opportunities, 2) the ability to identify, gather, measure, summarize, verify, analyze, and interpret financial and nonfinancial data that are useful for addressing the goals, problems, and opportunities, and 3) the ability to use data, exercise judgments, evaluate risks, and solve real-world problems. The focus should be on developing analytical and conceptual thinking, not on memorizing professional standards.

Professional Orientation

Accounting graduates should identify with the profession and be concerned with developing the knowledge, skills, and values of its members. They should know and understand the ethics of the profession and be able to make value-based judgments. They should be prepared to address issues with integrity, objectivity, competence, and concern for the public interest.

COURSES AND COURSE CONTENT

The overriding objective in developing course content should be to create a base upon which continued learning can be built. Professional accounting education has four components: general education, general business education, general accounting education, and specialized accounting education. The components can be addressed in a variety of ways. No one model of accounting education will be appropriate for all colleges and universities. Nevertheless, some minimum coverage of all four areas, including integration of the areas, should be part of the education of every accountant.

General Education

The curriculum for general education should develop in students the capacities for inquiry, abstract logical thinking, and critical analysis and should train them to understand and use quantitative data. It should improve their writing to the degree that they can perform at the level acceptable for professional accountants and should give them some awareness of the ingredients of sound research. It should develop speaking and listening skills, historical consciousness, international and multicultural knowledge, an appreciation of science, and the study of values and their role in decision-making. And it should include the esthetic experience. This goal will not be met by a random set of courses. Some structured set of courses is required, but the structure should not be overly restrictive.

General Business Education

Professional accountants must understand the environments in which they work. Accounting programs should therefore include courses designed to develop knowledge of the functional activities of business, government, and nonprofit organizations. The courses should cover finance, marketing, operations, organizational behavior, and how the general manager integrates all these functions.

The introductory accounting course should be given special attention. It must serve the interests of students who are not going to enter the profession as well as those who are. The broad approach recommended in these objectives serves the interests and needs of both groups. The course should teach, reinforce, and reward the skills, abilities, and attitudes that are necessary for success in the accounting profession. This will give students accurate knowledge about the nature of accounting careers, which will help them make a well informed choice about entering the profession.

General Accounting Education

Accounting courses should present accounting as an information development and communication process. The central theme should be how information is identified, measured, communicated, and used. The courses' essential components should be: 1) decision making and information in organizations, 2) design and use of information systems, 3) financial information and public reporting, including attestation, and 4) knowledge of the accounting profession. Courses should focus on both basic concepts and the application of these concepts in real-world environments, including international and ethical issues.

Specialized Accounting Education

Specialized accounting education should follow only after attainment of general accounting, organizational, and business knowledge. Therefore, it should be offered primarily at the post-baccalaureate level and via continuing education. Specialized accounting programs may include advanced study in financial accounting, management accounting, taxation, information systems, auditing, government (or nonprofit) accounting, and international accounting.

Continuing professional education may overlap considerably with specialized accounting education offered by universities. The principle of comparative advantage should govern which types of specializations are offered by universities and which by others.

INSTRUCTIONAL METHODS

The overriding objective of accounting programs should be to teach students to learn on their own. Therefore, accounting programs should not focus primarily on preparation for professional examinations. Students should be taught the skills and strategies that help them learn more effectively and how to use these effective learning strategies to continue to learn throughout their lifetimes.

Students must be active participants in the learning process, not passive recipients of information. They should identify and solve unstructured problems that require use of multiple information sources. Learning by doing should be emphasized. Working in groups should be encouraged. Creative use of technology is essential.

Accounting classes should not focus only on accounting knowledge. Teaching methods that expand and reinforce basic communication, intellectual, and interpersonal skills should be used.

Faculty must be trained to apply appropriate instructional methods. Doctoral programs therefore should give more attention to teaching methods. Faculty who are effective teachers and those who develop and implement new or innovative approaches to teaching and curriculum design should be recognized and rewarded for such scholarly activities.

Knowledge of historical and contemporary events affecting the profession is essential to effective teaching. It allows teachers to make lessons more relevant and to lend a real-world perspective to their classrooms. Faculty should therefore have current knowledge of the profession and its environment. Incentives should motivate faculty to be knowledgeable about and involved in the current professional accounting environment.

Instructional methods and materials need to change as the environment changes. Measurement and evaluation systems that encourage continuous updating and improvement of instructional methods and materials should be developed.

APPENDIX A

LEARNING TO LEARN

Learning is often defined and measured in terms of knowledge of facts, concepts, or principles. This "transfer of knowledge" approach to education has been the traditional focus of accounting education. One goal of the Accounting Education Change Commission is to change the educational focus from knowledge acquisition to "learning to learn", that is, developing in students the motivation and capacity to continue to learn outside the formal educational environment. Learning to learn involves developing skills and strategies that help one learn more effectively and to use these effective learning strategies to continue to learn throughout his or her lifetime.

Academic programs focused on teaching students how to learn must address three issues: 1) content, 2) process, and 3) attitudes.

The **content** of the program must create a base upon which continued learning can be built. Developing both an understanding of underlying concepts and principles and the ability to apply and adapt those concepts and principles in a variety of contexts and circumstances are essential to life-long learning. A focus on memorization of rules and regulations is contrary to the goal of learning to learn.

The **process** of learning should focus on developing the ability to identify problems and opportunities, search out the desired information, analyze and interpret the information, and reach a well reasoned conclusion. Understanding the process of inquiry in an unstructured environment is an important part of learning to learn.

Above all, an **attitude** of continual inquiry and life-long learning is essential for learning to learn. An attitude of accepting, even thriving on, uncertainty and unstructured situations should be fostered. An attitude of seeking continual improvement, both of self and the profession, will lead to life-long learning.

APPENDIX B

COMPOSITE PROFILE OF CAPABILITIES NEEDED
BY ACCOUNTING GRADUATES

1. General Knowledge
   - An understanding of the flow of ideas and events in history and the different cultures in today's world
   - Basic knowledge of psychology, economics, mathematics through calculus, and statistics
   - A sense of the breadth of ideas, issues, and contrasting economic, political and social forces in the world
   - An awareness of personal and social values and of the process of inquiry and judgment
   - An appreciation of art, literature, and science

2. Intellectual Skills
   - Capacities for inquiry, abstract logical thinking, inductive and deductive reasoning, and critical analysis
   - Ability to identify and solve unstructured problems in unfamiliar settings and to apply problem-solving skills in a consultative process
   - Ability to identify ethical issues and apply a value-based reasoning system to ethical questions
   - Ability to understand the determining forces in a given situation and to predict their effects
   - Ability to manage sources of stress by selecting and assigning priorities within restricted resources and to organize work to meet tight deadlines.

3. Interpersonal Skills
   - Ability to work with others, particularly in groups, to influence them, to lead them, to organize and delegate tasks, to motivate and develop people, and to withstand and resolve conflict
   - Ability to interact with culturally and intellectually diverse people.

4. Communication Skills
   - Ability to present, discuss, and defend views effectively through formal and informal, written and spoken language
   - Ability to listen effectively
   - Ability to locate, obtain, organize, report, and use information from human, print, and electronic sources

5. Organizational and Business Knowledge
   - A knowledge of the activities of business, government, and nonprofit organizations, and of the environments in which they operate, including the major economic, legal, political, social, and cultural forces and their influences

- A basic knowledge of finance, including financial statement analysis, financial instruments, and capital markets, both domestic and international
- An understanding of interpersonal and group dynamics in business
- An understanding of the methods for creating and managing change in organizations
- An understanding of the basic internal workings of organizations and the application of this knowledge to specific examples

6. Accounting Knowledge
   - History of the accounting profession and accounting thought
   - Content, concepts, structure, and meaning of reporting for organizational operations, both for internal and external use, including the information needs of financial decision makers and the role of accounting information in satisfying those needs
   - Policy issues, environmental factors, and the regulation of accounting
   - Ethical and professional responsibilities of an accountant
   - The process of identifying, gathering, measuring, summarizing, and analyzing financial data in business organizations, including:
     * The role of information systems
     * The concepts and principles of information system design and use
     * The methods and processes of information system design and use
     * The current and future roles of computer-based information technology
   - The concepts, methods, and processes of control that provide for the accuracy and integrity of financial data and safeguarding of business assets
   - The nature of attest services and the conceptual and procedural bases for performing them
   - Taxation and its impact on financial and managerial decisions
   - In-depth knowledge in one or more specialized areas, such as financial accounting, management accounting, taxation, information systems, auditing, nonprofit, government, and international accounting

7. Accounting Skills
   - Ability to apply accounting knowledge to solve real-world problems

8. Personal Capacities and Attitudes
   - Creative thinking
   - Integrity
   - Energy
   - Motivation
   - Persistence
   - Empathy
   - Leadership
   - Sensitivity to social responsibilities
   - A commitment of life-long learning

COMMISSION MEMBERS
1989-91

Doyle Z. Williams, Chairman
KPMG Peat Marwick Professor
University of Southern California

Gary L. Sundem, Executive Director
Bell Affiliate Program Professor
University of Washington

Steven Berlin
Vice President & CFO
Citgo Petroleum Corp.

John F. Chironna
President
BroadCom Inc.

Robert K. Elliott
Assistant to the Chairman
KPMG Peat Marwick

Nathan T. Garrett
Partner, Garrett and Davenport
Assistant Professor of Accounting and
 Law
North Carolina Central University

Charles T. Horngren
Edmund W. Littlefield Professor
 of Accounting
Stanford University

Donald E. Kieso
KPMG Peat Marwick Professor
Northern Illinois University

Paul L. Locatelli,S.J.
President
Santa Clara University

James L. Loebbecke
Kenneth A. Sorensen Peat Marwick
 Professor of Accounting
University of Utah

Melvin C. O'Connor
Professor of Accounting
Michigan State University

Vincent M. O'Reilly
Deputy Chairman
Coopers & Lybrand

Ray M. Sommerfeld
James L. Bayless/Rauscher
 Pierce Refsnes, Inc.
 Chair in Business Administration
University of Texas at Austin

Joan S. Stark
Professor of Education
Director of the National Center for
 Research to Improve Post
 Secondary Teaching and Learning
University of Michigan

A. Marvin Strait
Chairman
Strait, Kushinsky & Co.

Richard R. West
Dean
Leonard N. Stern School of
 Business
New York University

EX OFFICIO:

Rick Elam
Vice President, Education
American Institute of CPA's

Corine T. Norgaard
AAA Director of Education
Professor of Accounting
University of Connecticut

THE FIRST COURSE IN ACCOUNTING

Accounting Education Change Commission
Position Statement No. Two

June 1992

This Statement is issued by the Accounting Education Change Commission (AECC). The AECC was appointed in 1989 by the American Accounting Association and supported by the Sponsors' Education Task Force, representing the largest public accounting firms in the United States. Its objective is to be a catalyst for improving the academic preparation of accountants so that entrants to the accounting profession possess the skills, knowledge, and attitudes required for success in accounting career paths. This document may be copied without restriction.

THE FIRST COURSE IN ACCOUNTING

CONTENTS

THE FIRST COURSE IN ACCOUNTING

In its first Position Statement,[1] the Commission outlined the knowledge, skills, and orientation accounting graduates must possess to become successful professionals. This Statement builds upon that foundation by presenting the Commission's views on the first course in accounting.[2]

The concepts in this Statement apply directly to the first course in accounting at the undergraduate level. However, they are also applicable to courses in introductory accounting at the graduate level.

THE IMPORTANCE OF THE FIRST COURSE IN ACCOUNTING

The first course in accounting can significantly benefit those who enter business, government, and other organizations, where decision-makers use accounting information. These individuals will be better prepared for their responsibilities if they understand the role of accounting information in decision-making by managers, investors, government regulators, and others. All organizations have accountability responsibilities to their constituents, and accounting, properly used, is a powerful tool in creating information to improve the decisions that affect those constituents.

The first course has even more significance for those considering a career in accounting and those otherwise open to the option of majoring in accounting. The course shapes their perceptions of (1) the profession, (2) the aptitudes and skills needed for successful careers in

---

[1] Position Statement No. One: *Objectives of Education for Accountants* (September 1990). The views expressed in this Statement should be considered in conjunction with Position Statement No. One.

[2] "First course in accounting" refers to the introductory accounting sequence, usually taught over two terms (e.g.,introductory "financial" and "managerial" accounting).

accounting, and (3) the nature of career opportunities in accounting. These perceptions affect whether the supply of talent will be sufficient for the profession to thrive. For those who decide to major in accounting or other aspects of business, the course is an important building block for success in future academic work.

OBJECTIVE OF THE FIRST COURSE IN ACCOUNTING

The primary objective of the first course in accounting is for students to learn about accounting as an information development and communication function that supports economic decision-making. The knowledge and skills provided by the first course in accounting should facilitate subsequent learning even if the student takes no additional academic work in accounting or directly related disciplines. For example, the course should help students perform financial analysis; derive information for personal or organizational decisions; and understand business, governmental, and other organizational entities.

In achieving this objective, students completing the first course in accounting should--

■ Have a broad view of accounting's role in satisfying society's need for information and its function in business, in government, in other organizations, and in public accounting. Students should gain an overview of the accounting profession, encompassing its history, its ethics, its public responsibilities, and its international dimensions as well as an appreciation of the role of auditing in enhancing the credibility of publicly reported information.

■ Understand the basic features of accounting and reporting by organizations, including the principles underlying the design, integrity, and effectiveness of accounting information systems.

- Understand fundamental accounting concepts in additon to the elements of financial statements. These concepts include accountability, estimation, accounting judgment (for example, substance vs. form), the qualitative characteristics of accounting information, performance measurement (including productivity and quality), choice in accounting measurement (for example, defining profit centers and other units of accountability), accounting controls and processes, and the ethics of internal and external reporting.

- Appreciate the role of accounting in both the generation of taxes and preparation of economic measurements, by and for governmental bodies.

- Understand that some accounting systems are more effective than others in given circumstances and that the decision-usefulness of information produced by an accounting system depends on its design and choices among information capturing, analysis, and reporting options.

- Possess enchanced analytical skills and the ability to confront unstructured problems--that is, problems with more than one defensible solution.

- Gain an appreciation that accounting as a discipline is the focus of constructive debate and intensive re-thinking caused by economic and technological change, and one that will continue to evolve in the future.

In general, the first course in accounting should be an *introduction to accounting* rather than *introductory accounting*. It should be a rigorous course focusing on the relevance of accounting information to decision-making (use) as well as its source (preparation).

TEACHING METHODS

Teachers of the first course in accounting should put a priority on their interaction with students and on interaction among students. Students' involvement should be promoted by methods such as cases, simulations, and group projects. Emphasis should be on teaching the student to learn on his or her own.

FACULTY

The commitment of faculty resources[3] to the first course in accounting should be consistent with its foundational importance to the curriculum. The most effective instructors should teach the course. Those who teach the course should have a record of success in teaching, should have up-to-date knowledge of professional developments, should be able to support points by citing relevent research, should be able to bring an integrative organizational perspective to the course, and should be able to reinforce the relevance of the course to the students by examples from the non-academic work of the accounting profession. These qualifications should be supplemented by enthusiasm and commitments to teaching and the accounting profession.

CONCLUSION

The first course in accounting is very important to all who take it, whether they plan to become professional accountants or to use accounting information in non-accounting careers. If designed according to this Statement, the course can meet the educational needs of these

---

[3]Position Statement No. One: *Objectives of Education for Accountants* (September 1990), p.5, states, "Faculty who are effective teachers and those who develop and implement new or innovative approaches to teaching and curriculum design should be recognized and rewarded for such scholarly activities." See also Issues Statement No. 1: *AECC Urges Priority for Teaching in Higher Education* (August 1990).

students, engender accurate perceptions of the broad role of accounting in modern economies, and assist students in making well-informed career choices. The breadth of this influence increases the responsibility of every party capable of improving the effectiveness of the first course in accounting.

Other Statements issued by the Accounting Education Change Commission:

Issues Statement No.1: *AECC Urges Priority for Teaching in Higher Education* (August 1990).

Position Statement No. One: *Objectives of Education for Accountants* (September 1990).

Issues Statement No. 2: *AECC Urges Decoupling of Academic Studies and Professional Accounting Examination Preparation* (July 1991).

Issues Statement No. 3: *The Importance of Two-year Colleges for Accounting Education* (August 1992).

COMMISSION MEMBERS
1991-92

Doyle Z. Williams, Chairman
KPMG Peat Marwick Professor
of Accounting
University of Southern California

William G. Shenkir, Vice Chairman
Dean, McIntire School of Commerce
University of Virginia

Steve Berlin
Vice President & CEO
CITGO Petroleum Corp.

Sarah B. Blake
President & CEO
Technology Development
and Management Co.

John F. Chironna
President & CEO
BroadCom, Inc.

Robert K. Elliott
Assistant to the Chairman
KPMG Peat Marwick

Charles T. Horngren
Edmund W. Littlefield
Professor of Accounting
Stanford University

Donald E. Kieso
KPMG Peat Marwick
Professor of Accounting
Nortern Illinois University

David L. Landsittel
Managing Director-
Auditing Procedures
Arthur Anderson & Co.

Paul L. Locatelli, S.J.
President
Santa Clara University

James K. Laebbecke
Kenneth A. Sorensen
KPMG Peat Marwick
Professor of Accounting
University of Utah

Melvin C. O'Connor
Professor of Accounting
Michigan State University

Katherine Schipper
Professor of Accounting
University of Chicago

Ray M. Sommerfeld
James L. Bayless/Rauscher
Pierce Refsnes, Inc.
Chair in Business Administration
University of Texas at Austin

Joan S. Stark
Professor of Higher Education
University of Michigan

A. Marvin Strait
Chairman of the Board
Strait Kushinsky and Co., P.C.

EX OFFICIO:

Rick Elam
Vice President-Education
American Institute of
Certified Public Accounting

Robert W. Ingram
AAA Director of Education
Ernst & Young Professor of
Accounting
University of Alabama

AECC URGES PRIORITY FOR TEACHING IN HIGHER EDUCATION

Issues Statement No. I

August, 1990

This statement is issued by the Accounting Education Change Commission (AECC). The AECC was appointed in 1989 by the American Accounting Association and supported by the Sponsors' Education Task Force, representing the largest public accounting firms in the United States. Its objective is to be a catalyst for improving the academic preparation of accountants so that entrants to the accounting profession possess the skills, knowledge, and attitudes required for success in accounting career paths.

This statement has been endorsed by the Executive Committee of the American Accounting Association, the American Institute of Certified Public Accountants, Beta Alpha Psi, the Financial Executives Institute, the Federation of Schools of Accountancy, the Institute of Management Accountants, the California Society of Certified Public Accountants, the Colorado Society of Certified Public Accountants, Illinois Society of Certified Public Accountants, New York State Society of Certified Public Accountants, and the Texas Society of Certified Public Accountants.

AECC URGES PRIORITY FOR
TEACHING IN HIGHER EDUCATION

The Accounting Education Change Commission (AECC) recommends a redirected focus for higher education -- giving priority to teaching and curriculum and course development. The Commission urges accounting and business faculties to establish reward systems that reflect this priority. Giving teaching and curriculum and course development a more important role will require major changes in the recruitment, development, and evaluation of faculty members. The Commission is aware that these changes will be controversial. Nevertheless, it is convinced that an increased emphasis on teaching and curriculum and course development is vital to the future of accounting education.

A primary concern of the Commission is that the existing higher education reward structure does not reward teaching and curriculum and course development as favorably as other faculty pursuits. Educators who concentrate on teaching and curriculum and course development often are not appropriately rewarded and frequently face the risk of not gaining tenure. The so called "publish or perish" standard for promotion and tenure has created an environment that gives short shrift to virtually all non-research aspects of the educational process. Sufficient incentives must be provided to create an environment that rewards faculty for giving attention to teaching and related matters such as curriculum design, course development, and student interaction.

In calling for this shift in emphasis, the AECC joins others - such as the Carnegie Foundation for the Advancement of Teaching, the Irvine group, as well as prominent educators- in urging that teaching and curriculum and course development be given priority as universities allocate faculty and other resources. We are experiencing dramatic change in this "information age" and must adapt to the rapid pace in technology. Our ability to retain a competitive and viable society depends on our ability to educate. Accordingly, the importance of effective teaching and innovative curriculum and course development cannot be over emphasized.

University boards of trustees and/or regents can significantly influence the priorities of departments, colleges, and universities as they review and approve annual budgets. In state supported institutions, legislatures and governors can make a significant contribution by endorsing effective teaching and curriculum and course development as priorities. Clearly a shift in the allocation of resources to provide more support for teaching and curriculum and course development is a necessary condition for obtaining improvement in higher education.

Major supporters of higher education can have a significant influence in stimulating change. For instance, foundations, firms, corporations, and individuals that contribute money, offer grants, or fund specific academic programs should motivate change by requiring that substantial resources be directed toward the support of teaching and curriculum and course development.

The AECC encourages all who are interested in the future of the higher education to become involved in helping academia reorder its priorities and place renewed emphasis on teaching and curriculum and course development.

ACCOUNTING EDUCATION CHANGE COMMISSION
21515 Hawthorne Boulevard
Suite 1200 Union Bank Tower
Torrance, CA   90503-6503

COMMISSION MEMBERS
1989-91

Doyle Z. Williams, Chairman
KPMG Peat Marwick Professor
University of Southern California

Gary L. Sundem, Executive Director
Affiliate Program Professor
University of Washington

Steve Berlin
Vice President & CFO
CITGO Petroleum Corp.

John F. Chironna
President
BroadCom Inc.

Robert K. Elliott
Assistant to the Chairman
KPMG Peat Marwick

Nathan T. Garrett
Partner, Garrett and Davenport
Assistant Professor of Accounting and
  Law
North Carolina Central University

Charles T. Horngren
Edmund W. Littlefield Professor
  of Accounting
Stanford University

Donald E. Kieso
KPMG Peat Marwick Professor
Northern Illinois University

Paul L. Locatelli, S.J.
President
Santa Clara University

James K. Loebbecke
Kenneth A. Sorensen Peat Marwick
  Professor of Accounting
University of Utah

Melvin C. O'Connor
Professor of Accounting
Michigan State University

Vincent M. O'Reilly
Deputy Chairman
Coopers & Lybrand

Ray M. Sommerfeld
James L. Bayless/Rauscher
  Pierce Refsnes, Inc.
  Chair in Business Administration
University of Texas at Austin

Joan S. Stark
Professor of Education
Director of the National Center for
  Research to Improve Post Secondary
  Teaching and Learning
University of Michigan

A. Marvin Strait
Chairman
Strait, Kushinsky & Co.

Richard R. West
Dean
Leonard N. Stern School of Business
New York University

EX OFFICIO:

Rick Elam
Vice President - Education
American Institute of CPA's

Corine T. Norgaard
AAA Director of Education
Professor of Accounting
University of Connecticut

AECC URGES DECOUPLING OF ACADEMIC STUDIES AND PROFESSIONAL ACCOUNTING EXAMINATION PREPARATION

Issues Statement No.2

July 1991

This Statement is issued by the Accounting Education Change Commission (AECC). The AECC was appointed in 1989 by the American Accounting Association and supported by the Sponsors' Education Task Force, representing the largest public accounting firms in the United States. Its objective is to be a catalyst for improving the academic preparation of accountants so that entrants to the accounting profession possess the skills, knowledge, and attitudes required for success in accounting career paths.

AECC URGES DECOUPLING OF ACADEMIC STUDIES AND PROFESSIONAL ACCOUNTING EXAMINATION PREPARATION

The Accounting Education Change Commission (AECC) urges schools and students to maximize the educational opportunities provided by collegiate curricula. A primary concern of the Commission is the disruption in students' education caused by their taking examination review courses and engaging in other activities of a review nature in preparing to write professional examinations. Often students who take a professional examination near the conclusion of their college studies divert their efforts from their academic pursuits to preparing for such examinations. As a result, the full potential of the curriculum is not realized. Therefore, the Commission believes all activities that are primarily of a review nature designed for professional examination preparation should be deferred until the student has completed the education requirements of the respective examining agency.

The Commission also believes that degree credit should not be given for courses that are designed primarily to review for professional examinations. Curriculum objectives should be focused more broadly. Likewise, those organizations administering professional examinations, e.g., state boards of accountancy, should not recognize courses (1) for credit as part of the educational requirement to sit for the examination or (2) for awarding the certificate if those courses are offered primarily as a review of materials previously covered.

The Commission recognizes that implementing these changes may be controversial. Nevertheless, it is convinced that their implementation will enhance the quality of the educational experience of those preparing to enter the profession.

CPA EXAMINATION

The Accounting Education Change Commission recommends that candidates for the CPA Examination be required to complete their state's education requirements prior to applying to sit for the examination. The Commission urges State Boards of Accountancy and state legislative bodies in those states where such a requirement does not currently exist to amend the state board rules and/or state law as needed to achieve this objective.

The Commission believes that postponing applying to take the CPA Examination until the state's education requirements have been fulfilled will be beneficial in situations where schools complete the spring semester prior to the May examination. If candidates were merely required to complete the educational requirements prior to sitting for the CPA examination, the incentive to devote the final semester to prepping for the examination rather than to their academic pursuits would not be removed at these institutions. Further, requiring candidates to complete the jurisdiction's educational requirements prior to applying to sit for the examination may lessen the administrative burden on state boards.

In calling for this shift in timing in the preparation for the CPA Examination, the AECC is joined by the American Institute of Certified Public Accountants and the Uniformity of Regulation of the Accounting Profession Model Bill Task Force.

CMA EXAMINATION

The Institute of Certified Management Accountants of the Institute of Management Accountants (formerly the National Association of Accountants) allows students to apply for admission to the CMA program when they attain senior standing and to take the examination pending receipt of degree.

The Accounting Education Change Commission recommends that candidates for the CMA Examination be required to complete the ICMA's education, including degree, requirements prior to applying to sit for the examination.

CIA EXAMINATION

The Institute of Internal Auditors permits full-time students to apply to take the Certified Internal Auditors (CIA) Examination during the final year of their baccalaureate or graduate degree program and to take the examination immediately upon completion of their baccalaureate program.

The Accounting Education Change Commission recommends that candidates for the CIA Examination be required to complete the Institute of Internal Auditors' education, including degree, requirements prior to applying to sit for the examination.

ACCOUNTING EDUCATION CHANGE COMMISSION
21515 Hawthorne Boulevard
Suite 1200 Union Bank Tower
Torrance, CA 90503-6503

COMMISSION MEMBERS
1989-91

Doyle Z. Williams, Chairman
KPMG Peat Marwick
 Professor of Accounting
University of Southern California

Gary L. Sundem, Executive Director
Affiliate Program Professor
University of Washington

Steve Berlin
Vice President & CFO
CITGO Petroleum Corp.

John F. Chironna
President & CEO
BroadCom, Inc.

Robert K. Elliott
Assistant to the Chairman
KPMG Peat Marwick

Nathan T. Garrett
Partner, Garrett and Davenport
Assistant Professor of Accounting
 and Law
North Carolina Central University

Charles T. Horngren
Edmund W. Littlefield Professor
 of Accounting
Stanford University

Donald E. Kieso
KPMG Peat Marwick
 Professor of Accounting
Northern Illinois University

Paul L. Locatelli, S.J.
President
Santa Clara University

James K. Loebbecke
Kenneth A. Sorensen
 KPMG Peat Marwick
 Professor of Accounting
University of Utah

Melvin C. O'Connor
Professor of Accounting
Michigan State University

Vincent M. O'Reilly
Deputy Chairman
Coopers & Lybrand

Ray M. Sommerfeld
James L. Bayless/Rauscher
 Pierce Refsnes, Inc.
 Chair in Business Administration
University of Texas at Austin

Joan S. Stark
Professor of Higher Education
University of Michigan

A. Marvin Strait
Chairman of the Board
Strait Kushinsky and Company

Richard R. West
Dean
Leonard N. Stern School of Business
New York University

EX OFFICIO:

Rick Elam
Vice President--Education
American Institute of
 Certified Public Accountants

Corine T. Norgaard
AAA Director of Education
Professor of Accounting
University of Connecticut

THE IMPORTANCE OF TWO-YEAR COLLEGES FOR ACCOUNTING EDUCATION

Issues Statement No. 3

August 1992

This Statement is issued by the Accounting Education Change Commission (AECC). The AECC was appointed in 1989 by the American Accounting Association and supported by the Sponsors' Education Task Force, representing the largest public accounting firms in the United States. Its objective is to be a catalyst for improving the academic preparation of accountants so that entrants to the accounting profession possess the skills, knowledge, and attitudes required for success in accounting career paths. This document may be copied without restriction.

THE IMPORTANCE OF TWO-YEAR COLLEGES FOR ACCOUNTING EDUCATION

The Accounting Education Change Commission recognizes the important role of two-year colleges in accounting education. Over half of all students who take the first course in accounting do so at two-year colleges.[1] Approximately one-fourth of the students entering the accounting profession take their initial accounting coursework at two-year colleges. The proportion of students who begin their college educations at two-year colleges is increasing.[2] Therefore, the quality of education provided by two-year colleges has an important effect on the overall quality of accounting education.

The Commission encourages closer coordination between two and four-year colleges in the development of accounting curricula. Enhanced communication between accounting faculty and administrators at two-year and four-year colleges is likely to increase the quality of accounting education at both levels. By working together, accounting faculty at two-year and four-year colleges can understand better the backgrounds and expectations of their students. The better informed the faculty at the two-year colleges, the better they can help their students prepare for the programs to which they are going to transfer. A cooperative effort should attract better students to accounting.

Accounting administrators of two-year and four-year accounting programs should maintain contact with each other. Administrators at two-year colleges should identify four-year colleges to which their students transfer, and administrators at four-year colleges should identify two-year colleges from which their students transfer. Interactions through advisory boards, curricula committees, and joint faculty meetings should be encouraged.

---

[1] The Commission's opinion that the first course is critical to the quality of accounting education has been expressed in its Position Statement No. Two, *The First Course in Accounting.*

[2] These conclusions are based on results of surveys of members of the American Institute of Certified Public Accountants and Institute of Management Accountants and a survey of administrators of accounting programs at four-year schools by the Commission in the Spring, 1992.

Information about curricula, admissions, syllabi, and examinations should be exchanged to improve coordination of program requirements. Exchange of information is particularly important when curricula changes are considered. Sharing programs and materials designed to improve teaching, information about curriculum design and course development efforts, and ideas about how to recruit top students into accounting programs con enhance the quality of both two-year and four-year programs.

The Commission believes that the involvement of two-year colleges in accounting education change is critical for improving the overall quality of accounting education. It encourages greater recognition within the academic and professional communities of the efforts and importance of two-year accounting programs.

Previous Statements issued by the Accounting Education Change Commission:

Issues Statement No.1: *AECC Urges Priority for Teaching in Higher Education* (August 1990).

Position Statement No. One: *Objectives of Education for Accountants* (September 1990).

Issues Statement No. 2: *AECC Urges Decoupling of Academic Studies and Professional Accounting Examination Preparation* (July 1991).

Position Statement No. Two: *The First Course in Accounting* (June 1992).

ACCOUNTING EDUCATION CHANGE COMMISSION
21515 Hawthorne Boulevard
Suite 1250 Union Bank Tower
Torrance, CA 90503-6503

COMMISSION MEMBERS
1991-92

Doyle Z. Williams, Chairman
KPMG Peat Marwick Professor
 of Accounting
University of Southern California

William G. Shenkir, Vice Chairman
Dean, McIntire School of Commerce
University of Virginia

Steve Berlin
Vice President & CEO
CITGO Petroleum Corp.

Sarah G. Blake
President & CEO
Technology Development
 and Management Co.

John F. Chironna
President & CEO
BroadCom, Inc.

Robert K. Elliott
Assistant to the Chairman
KPMG Peat Marwick

Charles T. Horngren
Edmund W. Littlefield
 Professor of Accounting
Stanford University

Donald E. Kieso
KPMG Peat Marwick Professor
 of Accounting
Northern Illinois University

David L. Landsittel
Managing Director-
 Auditing Procedures
Arthur Andersen & Co.

Paul L. Locatelli, S.J.
President
Santa Clara University

James K. Loebbecke
Kenneth A. Sorensen
 KPMG Peat Marwick
 Professor of Accounting
University of Utah

Melvin C. O'Connor
Professor of Accounting
Michigan State University

Katherine Schipper
Professor of Accounting
University of Chicago

Ray M. Sommerfeld
James L. Bayless/Rauscher
 Pierce Refsnes, Inc.
 Chair in Business Administration
University of Texas at Austin

Joan S. Stark
Professor of Higher Education
University of Michigan

A. Marvin Strait
Chairman of the Board
Strait Kushinsky and Company

EX OFFICIO:

Rick Elam
Vice President--Education
American Institute of
 Certified Public Accountants

Robert W. Ingram
AAA Director of Education
Ernst & Young Professor of
 Accounting
University of Alabama

IMPROVING THE EARLY EMPLOYMENT EXPERIENCE OF ACCOUNTANTS

Accounting Education Change Commission
Issues Statement No. 4

April 1993

IMPROVING THE EARLY EMPLOYMENT EXPERIENCE OF ACCOUNTANTS

CONTENTS

This Statement is issued by the Accounting Education Change Commission (AECC). The AECC was appointed in 1989 by the American Accounting Association and supported by the Sponsors' Education Task Force, representing the largest public accounting firms in the United States. Its objective is to be a catalyst for improving the academic preparation of accountants so that entrants to the accounting profession possess the skills, knowledge, and attitudes required for success in accounting career paths. The Commission encourages reproduction and distribution of its statements.

IMPROVING THE EARLY EMPLOYMENT EXPERIENCE OF ACCOUNTANTS

The purpose of improving the academic preparation of accountants is to serve jointly the interests of accounting graduates, their employers, and those who rely on their work. This purpose is undone whenever the early employment experience discourages dedication to accounting as a career, dampens enthusiasm for life-long professional learning, or leads to performance beneath one's abilities. On the other hand, the same purpose is furthered by an experience that nourishes dedication, sparks enthusiasm, and improves abilities. Thus the early employment experience affects the productivity of educational assets acquired at colleges and universities. This is true of all career paths in accounting practice, whether in public accounting, in corporations, or in government and other nonprofit entities.

This Statement is directed to all the parties whose activities directly affect the early employment experience. Each can do a part to alleviate problems and improve results.

THE CURRENT EXPERIENCE

Recent studies indicate that many accounting graduates find that their early employment experience falls short of the expectations they had brought to the business world. Many find that their expectations butt head-on into unanticipated overtime, deadlines, budgets, diminished family time, job stress, and less-than-desired financial rewards. Although evidence shows that many young accountants appreciate the diversity of their job assignments, opportunities to develop business skills, technical challenges, and collegial experiences, unmet expectations nevertheless reduce the attractiveness of careers in the profession and of majors in accounting.

ECONOMIC CONSTRAINTS

The profession's economic environment constrains the options available to improve the early employment experience. Yet new hires, educated with the increased breadth this Commission believes necessary to prepare them for practice, will demand more of the early employment experience than have past graduates. Thus, despite economic constraints, the early employment experience must be addressed or it will get worse. The Commission believes it can be addressed through the practicable recommendations set out below.

RECOMMENDATIONS

Recommendations to improve the early employment experience cannot succeed unless they are in the interest of the parties that must take recommended actions. Fortunately, the parties who affect the early employment experience have an interest in improving it. This is most obvious in the case of students, but no less so in the case of employers. Satisfied personnel are more productive, and disgruntled personnel undermine the teamwork needed to perform today's accounting. Faculty are already engaged in helping students prepare for success in accounting careers. Measures that can help graduates prosper in the work environments they enter should therefore engage professors' interests and are consistent with the purposes of the curricular reform activity they are pursuing with the encouragement of this Commission.

The recommendations address students' preparation for the early employment experience, recruiting, and the early years of employment. An Appendix provides examples of how each recommendation might be effected.

Faculty members should --

■ Acquire and maintain a high level of knowledge about both practice issues and the nonacademic accountant's workplace.

■ Seek out opportunities to interact with practicing accountants.

■ Communicate knowledge about the conditions of practice to students.

Students should --

■ Seek opportunities to obtain first-hand knowledge of the business world and practice environment.

■ Obtain information about career opportunities and the job search.

Career planning and placement professionals should --

■ Organize career education programs.

■ Counsel students on career issues.

Recruiters should --

- Acquire and maintain high levels of knowledge about educational and early employment issues.

- Communicate accurately and fully about the early employment experience.

Supervisors of early work experience should --

- Provide strong leadership and mentoring for staff members.

- Build working conditions that are conducive to success.

- Provide challenging and stimulating work assignments.

Workplace educators of first- through third-year employees should --

- Select and design educational experiences based on knowledge of employees' needs.

- Reinforce important skills.

Employer management should --

- Acquire and maintain knowledge of the early employment experience.

- Promote working conditions that junior employees find attractive, nurturing, and stimulating.

- Help fulfill the other recommendations in this Statement.

CONCLUSION

The recommendations above make clear that all parties to the early employment experience can contribute to improving it. The Commission therefore urges all such parties to act on the recommendations addressed to them and to consider the advantages in taking such steps.

APPENDIX

EXAMPLES OF HOW THE PARTIES CAN EFFECT THE RECOMMENDATIONS

Faculty

Faculty members should acquire and maintain a high level of knowledge about practice issues and the nonacademic accountant's workplace.

- Read journals that cover changes in the practice environment.

- Participate in faculty internships (compensated employment as a professional accountant) that provide experience in current business and professional issues and decisionmaking.

- Request information from employers about the work environment.

- Attend recruiting events on campus and discuss issues with employers' representatives.

Faculty members should seek out opportunities to interact with practicing accountants.

- Become active in professional organizations that serve practitioners (for example, the American Institute of Certified Public Accountants, state CPA societies, the Institute of Management Accountants, the Financial Executives Institute, the Institute of Internal Auditors, and the Federal Government Accountants' Association).

- Instruct continuing professional education seminars and/or executive education sessions for employers.

- Invite practicing accountants and executives to participate in classes (including interactive discussions of practice issues).

- Attend employer-sponsored educational events to become knowledgeable about current issues.

- Visit employer organizations to become better acquainted with business issues and the work environment.

- Engage in cooperative research projects with practitioners on professional accounting issues.

Faculty members should communicate knowledge about the conditions of practice to students.

- Develop case materials for classroom use that convey a realistic picture of the practice environment.

- Incorporate information on the practice environment in other curricular materials. Familiarize students with the typical responsibilities of new employees and the need to be able to perform well when responsible for a part, rather than the whole, of a large project or engagement.

- Employ practicing accountants as adjunct professors to teach courses or parts of courses (this would also provide opportunities for faculty and practitioners to interact).

- Consider the role of student internships and cooperative work/study programs in accounting programs.

- Counsel students on the types of career opportunities in accounting and the kinds of information they should be obtaining at recruiting interviews.

- Because students generally will not have the opportunity to read this Statement, provide them with the recommendations for students below.

Students

Students should seek opportunities to obtain first-hand knowledge of the business world and practice environment.

- Seek internships, cooperative work/study arrangements, and summer employment opportunities that are broadly relevant to your likely career choice.[1] Students considering an accounting career should seek general business and

---

[1] The opportunities cited here include unpaid positions that instill relevant business or organizational knowledge.

organizational experience, not just accounting experience, because a key role of accounting is to support managerial decisionmaking.

■ Seek campus opportunities to build communication and business skills -- for example, serve as an officer of a campus organization.

Students should obtain information about career opportunities and the job search.

■ Become informed about career opportunities and the working conditions they provide. Since all professions have some entry-level experiences that are the counterpart of apprenticeship, compare conditions within professions in order to provide perspective.

■ Perform a critical assessment of the relationship between your aptitudes, interests, skills, and knowledge and those required by various career opportunities.

■ Student accounting organizations (for example, Beta Alpha Psi) should identify information that students should seek at recruiting interviews.

Career Planning and Placement Professionals

Career planning and placement professionals should organize career education programs.

■ Expose students to the full range of accounting career options.

■ Help establish internships and other short-term volunteer opportunities.

Career planning and placement professionals should advise and counsel students on career issues.

■ Help students integrate their knowledge of accounting careers and their knowledge of themselves.

■ Advise student accounting organization officers on appropriate speakers.

- Obtain industry information on working conditions and benefits (e.g., average compensation) and provide it to students.

Recruiters

Recruiters should acquire and maintain high levels of knowledge about educational and early employment issues.

- Keep abreast of curriculum and faculty changes at institutions that are recruiting sites and assess the degree to which these institutions are preparing students for your organization's work environment.

- Speak to recent hires in your organization before beginning the recruiting process to sensitize yourself to recent hires' concerns about working conditions and their careers.

- Know your organization's official position on educational and recruiting issues so that you avoid confusing students (and faculty) with inconsistent messages -- for example, about the types of graduates sought.

- Know the social and economic value of the work for which you are recruiting (for example, the audit's role in capital formation and capital cost reduction) so that you will not communicate confusion or doubt on this subject to those entering the profession.

Recruiters should communicate accurately and fully about the early employment experience.

- In communicating to the placement office, faculty, and potential hires, be realistic about the job opportunities and work environment at your organization and the characteristics sought in new hires.

- Be aware that the attitudes you convey in the recruiting process can affect graduates' early employment experiences.

- Never withhold information necessary to a reasonable appreciation of facts presented.

- Arrange when feasible to have interchanges between

potential recruits and younger members of your organization in circumstances permitting candor.

Supervisors of Early Work Experience

Supervisors should provide strong leadership and mentoring.

- Give frequent, honest, open, and interactive feedback to recent hires under your supervision.

- Listen to new or recent hires for indirect messages about their employment experience; when dissatisfaction is expressed, inquire directly about its nature and causes.

- Work to improve counseling and mentoring -- for example, by always acknowledging good performance, by treating employees under your supervision as individuals with careers (not just short-term tasks), by helping employees to understand their future opportunities, and by inquiring about their concerns and plans.

- Be a role model of a professional, conveying pride in your work and its importance to clients/customers and society.

Supervisors should build working conditions that are conducive to success.

- Inculcate a do-it-right-the-first-time mentality and create the conditions to help make it possible. For example, explain assignments thoroughly, allocate sufficient time to do high quality work, be open about any necessary constraints (including budgetary constraints), explain how assignments fit in with the "big picture," and supervise work to completion.

- Analyze your own experience as a new or recent hire and treat new or recent hires as you would have liked to be treated.

- Maintain a "level playing field" for your subordinates, fairly distributing the opportunities and burdens.

- Minimize job-related stress (realizing that recent hires are especially subject to stress and that you may be the source of it!).

Supervisors should provide challenging and stimulating work assignments.

■ Delegate responsibility to recent recruits as soon as they are ready to assume it.

■ Maximize your subordinates' opportunities to use verbal skills (both oral and written), critical thinking, and analytic techniques and help subordinates improve those skills.

Workplace Educators of First- Through Third-Year Employees

Workplace educators should select and design educational experiences based on knowledge of employees' needs.

■ Understand the demographics of those you are responsible to educate, including their prior education, experience, strengths, and deficiencies, and apply the knowledge in designing the curriculum.

■ Identify gaps between new hires' expectations and the experience offered by the organization and design the curriculum to help close them.

■ Work to ensure that employees are assigned to courses they need when they need them, including training-on-demand to the extent it is feasible.

■ Understand the employees' evolving job requirements and the organization's changing business needs, and adapt the curriculum in response.

Early employment education should reinforce important skills.

■ Design the curriculum to reinforce communication, interpersonal, and intellectual skills.

■ Provide all employees who direct the work of others, not just those at the management level, with skills in personnel management.

Employer Management

Management should acquire and maintain knowledge of the early employment experience.

- Apply techniques to assess the early-employment experiences of professionals in your organization (for example, use alumni surveys, morale surveys, employee focus groups, staff committees, and upward evaluation of superiors) and correct identified problems.

Management should promote working conditions that junior employees find attractive, nurturing, and stimulating.

- Match job content and skills, delegating work to the extent possible and assigning nonprofessional work to nonprofessionals.

- Consistently recognize outstanding performance.

- Implement programs that enhance mentoring opportunities (for example, big brother/sister programs).

- Install skill-based promotion and compensation systems (and avoid lockstep or time-in-grade systems).

Management should help fulfill the other recommendations in this Statement.

- Take responsibility for having your recruiters, supervisory personnel, and workplace educators follow the recommendations above.

- Create meaningful opportunities for interaction with faculty (e.g., internships).

- Create meaningful internship and/or work/study arrangements for interested students.

- Provide educational institutions with adequate information about your recruiting needs and the nature of your business and ensure that your own recruiters have such information.

- Communicate pride in the profession and the importance of its work.

The AECC acknowledges the contributions to the Statement of the following task force members who are not Commission members: James W. Deitrick, Brian J. Jemelian, and Jean C. Wyer.

Other Statements issued by the Accounting Education Change Commission:

Issues Statement No. 1: *AECC Urges Priority for Teaching in Higher Education* (August 1990).

Position Statement No. One: *Objectives of Education for Accountants* (September 1990).

Issues Statement No. 2: *AECC Urges Decoupling of Academic Studies and Professional Accounting Examination Preparation* (July 1991).

Position Statement No. Two : *The First Course in Accounting* (June 1992).

Issues Statement No. 3: *The Importance of Two-Year Colleges for Accounting Education* (August 1992).

Issues Statement No. 5: *Evaluating and Rewarding Effective Teaching* (April 1993).

COMMISSION MEMBERS
1992-93

Doyle Z. Williams, Chairman
KPMG Peat Marwick Professor
   of Accounting
University of Southern California

William G. Shenkir, Vice Chairman
William Stamps Farish Professor
   of Free Enterprise
McIntire School of Commerce
University of Virginia

Sarah G. Blake
President & CEO
Technology Management and
   Developement, Inc.

John F. Chironna
President & CEO
BroadCom, Inc.

Robert K. Elliott
Assistant to the Chairman
KPMG Peat Marwick

Penny A. Flugger
Senior Vice President and Auditor
J.P. Morgan & Co. Incorporated

Donald E. Kieso
KPMG Peat Marwick Professor
   of Accountancy
Northern Illinois University

David L. Landsittel
Managing Director - Auditing
   Procedures
Arthur Andersen & Co.

Paul L. Locatelli, S.J.
President
Santa Clara University

Gerhard G. Mueller
Senior Associate Dean and
   Professor of Accounting
University of Washington

Melvin C. O'Connor
Professor of Accounting
Michigan State University

Katherine Schipper
Professor of Accounting
University of Chicago

Joan S. Stark
Professsor of Higher Education
University of Michigan

A. Marvin Strait
Chairman of the Board
Strait Kushinsky and Company

G. Peter Wilson
Associate Professor of
   Business Administration
Harvard University

Robert E. Witt
Dean, College of Business
   Administration and Graduate
   School of Business
The University of Texas at Austin

EX OFFICIO:

Rick Elam
Vice President-Education
American Institute of
   Certified Public Accountants

Robert W. Ingram
AAA Director of Education
Ernst & Young Professor of
   Accounting
University of Alabama

EVALUATING AND REWARDING EFFECTIVE TEACHING

Accounting Education Change Commission
Issues Statement No. 5

April 1993

EVALUATING AND REWARDING EFFECTIVE TEACHING

CONTENTS

This Statement is issued by the Accounting Education Change Commission (AECC). The AECC was appointed in 1989 by the American Accounting Association and supported by the Sponsors' Education Task Force, representing the largest public accounting firms in the United States. Its objective is to be a catalyst for improving the academic preparation of accountants so that entrants to the accounting profession possess the skills, knowledge, and attitudes required for success in accounting career paths. The Commission encourages reproduction and distribution of its statements.

EVALUATING AND REWARDING
EFFECTIVE TEACHING

The Commission's first Position Statement, on the objectives of education for accountants, emphasized the importance of teaching. The Statement cited the need for training in instructional methods, recognizing and rewarding contributions to teaching and curriculum design, and measurement and evaluation systems that encourage continuous improvement of instructional methods and materials.[1] Without progress in these prerequisites to effective teaching, the objectives of that Statement cannot be realized. Moreover, progress is needed in mechanisms for sharing ideas and techniques and in the culture and organizational climate that establishes and maintains the scholarly status of teaching within the professoriate.

All interested parties (e.g., university boards of trustees, regents, legislatures, governors, parents of students, and other sponsors of education) should help establish a priority on teaching and otherwise improve its effectiveness, but faculty and administrative leaders bear the greatest responsibility.

CHARACTERISTICS OF EFFECTIVE TEACHING

The characteristics of effective teaching must be identified if their presence is to be measured and improvements envisioned. Understanding the characteristics of effective teaching is essential for faculty (so they know what is expected) and administrators (so they can assess performance). Five characteristics of effective teaching are listed below.

■ **Curriculum Design and Course Development.** To effectively design curricula and develop courses the teacher must: set appropriate objectives; develop a useful framework for the conduct of courses and programs; conceptualize, organize, and properly sequence the subject matter; integrate courses with other related courses, disciplines, and current research; and be innovative and adaptive to change.

■ **Use of Well Conceived Course Materials.** Effective course materials enhance presentation skills, fulfill course objectives, are consistent with current developments and new technology in the field, create a base upon which continued learning can be built, challenge students to think, and give them the tools to solve problems.

---

[1] Position Statement No. One: *Objectives of Education for Accountants* (September, 1990).

■ **Presentation Skills.** Effective presentation skills stimulate students' interests and their active participation in the learning process, respond to classroom developments as they occur, convey mastery of the subject matter, achieve clarity of exposition, instill professionalism, and engage students with different learning styles.

■ **Well Chosen Pedagogical Methods and Assessment Devices.** Effective pedagogical methods (e.g., experiments, cases, small group activities) vary with circumstances (e.g., size of class, nature of the subject, ability or skill being developed). Assessment devices (e.g., examinations, projects, papers, presentations) should be geared both to course objectives and to the progress of the course and should have a pedagogical component (e.g., fixing in the student's mind what is most important, learning by thinking through a problem, identifying weaknesses to be corrected, reinforcing acquired skills).

■ **Guidance and Advising.** An effective teacher guides and advises students as appropriate to the level of study and research (e.g., a freshman's exploration of potential careers, a senior's job placement, or a doctoral student's work on a dissertation).

THE ADMINISTRATIVE TASK

Administrators should ensure that the reward structure stimulates effective teaching. They should also give attention to the other administrative issues that can affect the quality of teaching. These include:

■ The school's or department's infrastructure for learning. This infrastructure includes, for example, classrooms, EDP and projection equipment, library facilities, and study space.

■ Deployment of discretionary resources (e.g., availability of secretarial assistance, printing and duplicating, travel funds for teaching conferences).

■ Appropriate class sizes and teaching loads, given the educational mission and resources of the school.

Administrators should consider how each of the factors above is influencing the quality of teaching at their institutions and whether improvements can be made. Finally, administrators should be satisfied with the quality of the procedures in place in their institutions to evaluate teaching and continuously improve it.

REWARDING EFFECTIVE TEACHING

Faculty and administrators have a joint responsibility to develop incentive systems that produce the best educational outcomes for students. No one reward system or set of reward criteria can serve all institutions, but all should create adequate incentives for effective teaching. The incentive systems should reward effective teaching in deed as well as in word. Effective teaching should be a primary consideration in the tenure, promotion, and merit evaluation process. Effectiveness and innovation are not free, and it would be a mistake to assume that in the long term simply faculty pride and altruism are sufficient to accomplish continual change and improvement in the instructional function.

STRATEGIES FOR EVALUATING AND IMPROVING TEACHING

There is a close relationship between evaluating and improving teaching. Information about performance provides feedback on where improvements might be made. Assessments of performance need not have a purely administrative function of determining salaries and promotions; they can be devoted to improving teaching. The techniques below illustrate the range of what is available. Regardless of the technique chosen, assessments of teaching should be systematic and consistent.

- **Self-assessment.** Every teacher should regularly assess his or her work in order to improve. Self-assessment requires an evaluation of what was effective, what was not, why some things were relatively more effective, and what changes are desirable. Self-assessments can include documentation of purposes and techniques provided to colleagues as part of formal evaluations and are a natural basis for informal discussions of teaching techniques.

- **Observations by Colleagues.** Faculty should be primarily responsible for evaluating the teaching performance of colleagues. The evaluation process should be systematic and should strive for objectivity. A structured approach lends consistency to observations, which can make subsequent observations less stressful. All observations by colleagues should have as a major purpose to make recommendations for improvement, even if the occasion for the observation is administrative. Experience should be considered in assigning faculty observers.

- **Student Evaluations.** Student evaluations provide direct evidence of student attitudes toward the classroom experience. Students can report reactions to course workload; to the course materials; to the teacher's classroom enthusiasm, demeanor, and control; and to their personal interaction with the teacher. They can also estimate their own academic growth in the course.

- **Alumni Input.** Graduates can report on the thoroughness of their preparation, the usefulness of specific educational experiences in their lives and careers, and recollections of effective courses and teachers. Aggregate data on alumni outcomes (e.g., employment data) can be combined with information on curriculum design and teaching effectiveness to evaluate how both an accounting program and teaching approaches might be improved.

- **Instructional Consultants.** Consultants can analyze teaching techniques and styles and provide recommendations for improvement. Sometimes it is useful to work with a consultant and a faculty colleague, with the colleague focusing on course content and the consultant on teaching techniques.

- **Teaching Portfolios.** A teaching portfolio is a factual description or collection of a professor's teaching achievements (i.e., an extended teaching resume). The teaching portfolio is to a professor's teaching what lists of publications, grants, and academic honors are to research. A portfolio might include documentation of one's teaching experience and philosophy, syllabi, evidence of student learning, student and faculty evaluations, videotapes, and documentation of work on curriculum design and course development. A teaching portfolio may be critical to providing the teaching vita with the portability and external review enjoyed for so long by the publishing vita.

CONCLUSION

Every party with a stake in improving accounting education has a stake in improving accounting professors' teaching, but faculty and administrators can do the most to bring it about. They can work to ensure that teaching is appropriately rewarded and supported, that campus conditions are conducive to effective teaching, that effective teaching strategies are shared with others, that sound mechanisms for feedback on teaching effectiveness are in place and functioning, and that methods of evaluating teaching are refined and are viewed as credible by those who play key roles in the evaluation and reward process.

SELECTED BIBLIOGRAPHY

Angelo, Thomas A. and K. Patricia Cross. *Classroom Assessment Techniques: A Handbook for College Teachers* (2nd Edition) San Francisco, CA: Jossey-Bass Publishers, 1993

Boyer, Ernest L. *Scholarship Reconsidered: Priorities of the Professoriate.* Princeton, N.J.: The Carnegie Foundation for the Advancement of Teaching, 1990.

Blackburn, Robert T. and Judith A. Pitney. *Performance Appraisal for Faculty: Implications for Higher Education.* Ann Arbor, MI: National Center for Research to Improve Postsecondary Education, The University of Michigan, 1988.

Braskamp, Larry A. and John C. Ory. *Assessing Faculty Work.* San Francisco, CA: Jossey-Bass Publishers (in preparation), 1993.

Cashin, William E. "Defining and Evaluating College Teaching," *IDEA Paper No. 21.* Kansas State University, Center for Faculty Evaluation and Development, September 1989.

Centra, John, Robert C. Froh, Peter J. Gray, Leo M. Lambert and Robert M. Diamond., eds. *A Guide to Evaluating Teaching for Promotion and Tenure.* Syracuse University, Center for Instructional Development, 1987.

Diamond, Robert M. *Designing and Improving Courses and Curricula in Higher Education.* San Francisco: Jossey-Bass Publishers, 1989.

Edgerton, Russell, Patricia Hutchings and Kathleen Quinlan. *The Teaching Portfolio: Capturing the Scholarship in Teaching.* Washington, D.C.: American Association for Higher Education, 1991.

Gabbin, Alexander L., Scott N. Cairns and Ralph L. Benke, Jr., eds. *Faculty Performance Appraisal.* Harrisonburg VA: Center for Research in Accounting Education, 1990.

Lambert, Leo M. and Stacey Lane Tice, eds. *Preparing Graduate Students to Teach: A Guide to Programs that Improve Undergraduate Education and Develop Tomorrow's Faculty.* Washington, D.C.: American Association of Higher Education, 1993.

McKeachie, Wilbert J. *Teaching Tips: A Guide Book for the Beginning College Teacher.* (8th Edition) Lexington, MA: Heath and Company, 1986.

McKeachie, Wilbert J., Paul R. Pintrich, Yi-Guang Lin and David Smith. *Teaching and Learning in the College Classroom: A Review of the Research Literature.* Ann Arbor, MI: National Center for Research to Improve Postsecondary Education, The University of Michigan, 1986.

Menges, Robert J. and B. Claude Matkis, eds. *Key Resources on Teaching, Learning, Curriculum, and Faculty Development.* San Francisco, CA: Jossey-Bass Publishers, 1988.

Seldin, Peter. *The Teaching Portfolio: A Practical Guide to Improved Performance and Promotion Tenure Decisions.* Boston, MA: Anker Publishing, 1991.

Seldin, Peter and others. *How Administrators Can Improve Teaching: Moving from Talk to Action in Higher Education.* San Francisco, CA: Jossey-Bass Publishers, 1990.

Stark, Joan S. and others. *Planning Introductory College Courses: Influences on Faculty.* Ann Arbor, MI: National Center for Research to Improve Postsecondary Education, The University of Michigan, 1990.

St. Pierre, E. Kent, Michael P. Riordan and Diane A. Riordan., eds. *Research in Instructional Effectiveness.* Harrisonburg, VA: Center for Research in Accounting Education, 1990.

The Teaching Professor. A newsletter published by Magna Publications, Inc., Madison, WI: Maryellen G. Weimer, Editor, Pennsylvania State University.

The AECC acknowledges the contributions to the Statement of the following task force members who are not Commission members: Ronald J. Patten and Arthur R. Wyatt.

Other Statements issued by the Accounting Education Change Commission:

Issues Statement No. 1: *AECC Urges Priority for Teaching in Higher Education* (August 1990).

Position Statement No. One: *Objectives of Education for Accountants* (September 1990).

Issues Statement No. 2: *AECC Urges Decoupling of Academic Studies and Professional Accounting Examination Preparation* (July 1991).

Position Statement No. Two: *The First Course in Accounting* (June 1992).

Issues Statement No. 3: *The Importance of Two-Year Colleges for Accounting Education* (August 1992).

Issues Statement No. 4: *Improving the Early Employment Experience of Accountants* (April 1993).

COMMISSION MEMBERS
1992-93

Doyle Z. Williams, Chairman
KPMG Peat Marwick Professor
   of Accounting
University of Southern California

William G. Shenkir, Vice Chairman
William Stamps Farish Professor
   of Free Enterprise
McIntire School of Commerce
University of Virginia

Sarah G. Blake
President & CEO
Technology Management and
   Developement, Inc.

John F. Chironna
President & CEO
BroadCom, Inc.

Robert K. Elliott
Assistant to the Chairman
KPMG Peat Marwick

Penny A. Flugger
Senior Vice President and Auditor
J.P. Morgan & Co. Incorporated

Donald E. Kieso
KPMG Peat Marwick Professor
   of Accountancy
Northern Illinois University

David L. Landsittel
Managing Director - Auditing
   Procedures
Arthur Andersen & Co.

Paul L. Locatelli, S.J.
President
Santa Clara University

Gerhard G. Mueller
Senior Associate Dean and
   Professor of Accounting
University of Washington

Melvin C. O'Connor
Professor of Accounting
Michigan State University

Katherine Schipper
Professor of Accounting
University of Chicago

Joan S. Stark
Professsor of Higher Education
University of Michigan

A. Marvin Strait
Chairman of the Board
Strait Kushinsky and Company

G. Peter Wilson
Associate Professor of
   Business Administration
Harvard University

Robert E. Witt
Dean, College of Business
   Administration and Graduate
   School of Business
The University of Texas at Austin

EX OFFICIO:

Rick Elam
Vice President-Education
American Institute of
   Certified Public Accountants

Robert W. Ingram
AAA Director of Education
Ernst & Young Professor of
   Accounting
University of Alabama

TRANSFER OF ACADEMIC CREDIT FOR THE FIRST COURSE IN ACCOUNTING BETWEEN TWO-YEAR AND FOUR-YEAR COLLEGES

Accounting Education Change Commission
Issues Statement No. 6

The AECC acknowledges the contributions to the Statement of the following Task Force members who are not Commission members: Linda Lessing, Paul Solomon, and Mary Tharp.

This Statement is issued by the Accounting Education Change Commission (AECC). The AECC was appointed in 1989 by the American Accounting Association and supported by the Sponsors' Education Task Force, representing the largest public accounting firms in the United States. Its objective is to be a catalyst for improving the academic preparation of accountants so that entrants to the accounting profession possess the skills, knowledge, and attitudes required for success in accounting career paths. The Commission encourages reproduction and distribution of its statements.

TRANSFER OF ACADEMIC CREDIT
FOR THE FIRST COURSE IN ACCOUNTING
BETWEEN TWO-YEAR AND FOUR-YEAR COLLEGES

In its Issues Statement No. 3,[1] the Commission recognized "the important role of two-year colleges in accounting education" and noted that "approximately one-fourth of the students entering the accounting profession take their initial accounting coursework at two-year colleges." Because the number of students who begin their accounting education at two-year colleges is large and increasing, the transferability of academic credit for the "first course in accounting"[2] from two-year to four-year colleges is a matter of substantial concern to both students and accounting educators. Transferability of credit for the first course in accounting between two-year and four-year colleges continues to require close coordination by the respective institutions.

The Commission has envisioned and urged adoption of a new approach for the teaching of accounting. Accordingly, in Position Statement No. Two, the Commission stated that "the primary objective of the first course in accounting is for students to learn about accounting as an information development and communication function that supports economic decision-making." The new approach is very different in both course content and pedagogy (delivery) from the "conventional" approach. As long as some programs continue to offer the conventional course while others adopt the Commission's objective for their course, special efforts must be taken to ensure that students are able to transfer credit for the course from two-year to four-year colleges.

During this time of change in the introductory accounting sequence as envisioned by the Commission, two potential problematic relationships may develop for students who seek to transfer credit for the course: first, students of a two-year college who take a course that follows the Commission's "Objective" approach may transfer to a four-year college offering the "conventional" approach; second, students of a two-year college who take a "conventional" course may transfer to a four-year college offering a course meeting the Commission's "Objective" for the first course. The situation is even more complex if students from a given two-year college transfer their credits to several four-year colleges, which differ in how, and the extent to which, they are redesigning their accounting

---

[1]Accounting Education Change Commission, Issues Statement No. 3: *The Importance of Two-Year Colleges for Accounting Education* (August 1992).

[2]As noted in the Commission's Position Statement No. Two, " 'First Course in Accounting' refers to the introductory accounting sequence, usually taught over two years (e.g., introductory 'financial' and 'managerial' accounting)." [Accounting Education Change Commission, Position Statement No. Two: *The First Course in Accounting* (June 1992).]

curricula. Similar issues arise in relations among four-year schools, and a substantial portion of this document applies to those situations as well.

Renegotiating transferability agreements to focus on skills and knowledge (sometimes called student outcomes) and activities intended to develop the agreed-upon set of skills and knowledge is one approach to assuring transfer of academic credit for the introductory accounting sequence in the face of episodic or continual curriculum change. To begin such renegotiations, faculty at the affected institutions should develop a general statement of what skills and knowledge should be developed in the introductory accounting sequence. (Alternatively, such statements could be developed through state or regional cooperative efforts.) Appendix A contains more information about this approach.

Faculty at a two-year college who wish to redesign their introductory accounting sequence might consider the questions and process outlined in Appendix B to assist in coordinating the anticipated change with the four-year colleges to which their students transfer. Similarly, if the curriculum change process begins first at a four-year college with transferability agreements, the involved faculty should invite colleagues at the two-year colleges where such agreements are in place, to work together to renegotiate the agreements in a way that facilitates the continued transfer of academic credit for the introductory accounting sequence.

APPENDIX A[3]

STUDENT COMPETENCIES AS A BASIS FOR TRANSFERABILITY AGREEMENTS

This appendix suggests one possible approach to transferability agreements for the introductory accounting sequence. Under the approach described in this appendix, four-year and two-year colleges would develop transferability agreements based on competencies implied by the Commission's Position Statement No. Two, *The First Course in Accounting.* The Statement suggests three categories of competencies: financial accounting, managerial accounting, and active learning.

A competency based approach to transferability agreements is likely to have two effects which differ from those of a textbook/topic approach. First, the textbook no longer dictates the organization and coverage of the course. Instead, the desired outcomes (skills and knowledge) become the driver and the textbook becomes one of possibly several vehicles. Second, the course is driven by an output measure (skills and knowledge to be achieved) rather than an input measure (textbook/ topics).

One example is provided of a desired outcome in each category (financial accounting, managerial accounting, and active learning) with possible activities designed to achieve each outcome:

1. Financial accounting:

    <u>Accounting's role in society</u>

    A. How does accounting meet the information needs of investors and creditors?

        (1) identify the types of decisions investors and creditors make and describe what information in the financial statements and/or related disclosures meets the information needs of each group

        (2) discuss what role ethics plays in the preparation of financial statements

        (3) identify and discuss examples of how U.S. accounting measurement techniques and financial state-

---

[3]This appendix is based on the recent work of a California Society of CPAs Task Force and its work product entitled "The California Core Competency Model for the First Course in Accounting" (May 12, 1995).

ments differ from the measurement techniques and financial statements of other countries

B. How does accounting meet the information needs of regulatory agencies and taxing authorities?

   (1) describe how information sources other than the annual report (e.g., SEC Form 10-K) can be used to learn more about the nature of an entity's business

   (2) identify some of the differences between the objectives of tax accounting and financial accounting and at least one difference between taxable income and financial accounting income

   (3) explain how a tax return is actually a special version of the income statement

2. Managerial accounting:

Role of the management accountant

A. How does management accounting differ from financial accounting and what role does the management accountant play as a member of the management team?

   (1) distinguish between the usefulness of managerial and financial accounting by considering the activities of planning, evaluating, controlling, and decision making

   (2) explain why managerial accounting applies to all types of industries (e.g., merchandising, manufacturing, non-financial services, financial services, government and other nonprofit entities)

   (3) describe different ways in which the management accountant's advice can help an entity to operate more effectively

   (4) analyze a company's financial statements and/or management reports and identify several strengths and several weaknesses of the company from this analysis

B. Why do management accountants need to have both a broad and in-depth understanding of their entity to fully participate in decisions about the products and services provided?

 (1) discuss, using specific examples, the cause and effect relationship between expenses and revenues and how they affect operating decisions

 (2) discuss the need for and uses of a management control system and how accounting information facilitates control

 (3) explain how the operating philosophies of continuous improvement, total quality management, and just-in-time manufacturing are used to manage optimal inventory levels, and discuss how the accounting function can be used to support their implementation

3. Active Learning:

 Group work skills (How can students demonstrate their ability to work effectively in groups?)

 A. Participate in groups whose task is to do one or more of the following:

 (1) solve problems
 (2) discuss readings from the financial press
 (3) analyze financial statements
 (4) analyze case studies

 B. Perform the following tasks that are commonly associated with collaborative or cooperative learning:

 (1) facilitate the discussion and keep the group on task
 (2) record the group's results
 (3) report the results of the group's work to the class
 (4) keep time, assist the leader, and fill vacant roles

SUGGESTIONS FOR TWO-YEAR COLLEGE FACULTY WHO WISH TO REDESIGN THE INTRODUCTORY ACCOUNTING SEQUENCE

This appendix uses a series of questions to outline a process that a two-year college faculty might consider in redesigning the introductory accounting sequence while preserving transferability of academic credit for the new course(s) to four-year colleges. The appendix is included here to share a process that was used successfully by a two-year college to initiate efforts to redesign the introductory accounting sequence.

What four-year colleges should be directly involved in the redesign?

Review student transfer information at the two-year college to determine the transfer (four-year) institutions having the greatest number of transfer students from your institution. Determine whether one of the four-year colleges is critical in determining course credit transferability. If that particular four-year college accepts your curriculum changes, will the other four-year colleges receiving your students most likely do so as well?

Who should be involved in the process?

Determine who makes the transfer credit decisions in the relevant four-year colleges. If the decisions are made by an administrative department, direct involvement of an influential and sympathetic accounting faculty member from the four-year institution may be very helpful, perhaps even necessary, to gaining acceptance for the proposed changes.

How is the transfer agreement to be achieved?

If the four-year colleges to which your students transfer are redesigning their accounting curriculum, you may wish to seek involvement in the four-year institution's change process. Alternatively, faculty at the two-year school can initiate the change, perhaps by inviting one or more faculty members of the four-year institution to join the two-year college's advisory committee.

Determine what curriculum changes might be most desired by, or at least acceptable to, the four-year institutions. For example, if course content has been the primary criterion to determine the transferability of academic credit courses, changes that shift the emphasis to the use of accounting information for decision making with little or no change in the topical content might be acceptable.

Assess how critical thinking skills, learning-to-learn skills, and communication skills may be incorporated into the new introductory accounting sequence, or taught in other courses, with specific applications incorporated into the introductory sequence in accounting. Delivery methods and student responsibilities could be changed to accomplish this.

Keep in mind that accounting majors need to develop an understanding of the accounting process of collecting and summarizing information and preparation of accounting reports. These majors may need to take an additional lab or mini-course in order to cover this material.

While two-year college faculty should remain flexible and open to compromise, any redesign of their introductory sequence in accounting should accomplish their agreed-upon objectives. If the transfer institution insists on dictating all of the changes, then the two-year faculty should attempt to use whatever flexibility remains to incorporate their desired changes into the transfer institution's requirements. Sometimes it is possible to achieve improved results by approaching a given topic with a different teaching methodology.

How might the final articulation agreement be accomplished?

As input to your final proposal, seek the counsel of an advisory committee, which might include local business and professional representatives as well as four-year college faculty. Ask to present the new course proposal to the accounting faculty of four-year institutions to which your students transfer and invite their input. Ask any faculty member from a four-year institution who might be serving on the advisory committee to brief the administrative department at the four-year institution that handles transferability of course credits.

Other Statements issued by the Accounting Education Change Commission:

Issues Statement No. 1: *AECC Urges Priority for Teaching in Higher Education* (August 1990).

Position Statement No. One: *Objectives of Education for Accountants* (September 1990).

Issues Statement No. 2: *AECC Urges Decoupling of Academic Studies and Professional Accounting Examination Preparation* (July 1991).

Position Statement No. Two: *The First Course in Accounting* (June 1992).

Issues Statement No. 3: *The Importance of Two-Year Colleges for Accounting Education* (August 1992).

Issues Statement No. 4: *Improving the Early Employment Experience of Accountants* (April 1993).

Issues Statement No. 5: *Evaluating and Rewarding Effective Teaching* (April 1993).

COMMISSION MEMBERS
1994-95

Gerhard G. Mueller, Chairman
Senior Associate Dean and
   Professor of Accounting
University of Washington

Richard E. Flaherty, Executive Director
Professor of Accounting
Arizona State University

Sarah G. Blake
President & CEO
Technology Management and
   Development, Inc.

Penny A. Flugger
Managing Director
J. P. Morgan & Co. Inc.

Barron H. Harvey
Dean, School of Business
Howard University

David L. Landsittel
Managing Director - Auditing
   Procedures
Arthur Andersen & Co. LLP

Paul L. Locatelli, S.J.
President
Santa Clara University

James Naus
Managing Partner
Crowe, Chizek

Melvin C. O'Connor
Professor of Accounting
Michigan State University

David B. Pearson
National Director of Audit
   Quality Control
Ernst & Young LLP

Stanley R. Pylipow
Advisor to Closely-Held
   Businesses

R. Eugene Rice
Scholar in Residence and Director,
Forum on Faculty Roles and Rewards
American Assoc. of Higher Education

Katherine Schipper
Professor of Accounting
University of Chicago

William G. Shenkir
William Stamps Farish Professor
   of Free Enterprise
University of Virginia

G. Peter Wilson
Visiting Associate Professor
Massachusetts Institute of Technology

Robert E. Witt
Dean, College of Business
University of Texas at Austin

EX OFFICIO:

Rick Elam
Vice President - Education
American Institute of Certified
   Public Accountants

Jan R. Williams
AAA Director of Education
Ernst & Young Professor of Accounting
University of Tennessee